Awesome Asian Animals

A+ books

Orangutans Are Awesome!

by Allan Morey

Consultant: Jackie Gai, DVM
Wildlife Vet

raintree
a Capstone company — publishers for children

Raintree is an imprint of Capstone Global Library Limited, a company incorporated in England and Wales having its registered office at 7 Pilgrim Street, London, EC4V 6LB – Registered company number: 6695582

www.raintree.co.uk
myorders@raintree.co.uk

Edited by Michelle Hasselius
Designed by Peggie Carley
Picture research by Tracy Cummins
Production by Morgan Walters
Printed and bound in China.

ISBN 978-1-474-70253-9
19 18 17 16 15
10 9 8 7 6 5 4 3 2 1

British Library Cataloguing in Publication Data
A full catalogue record for this book is available from the British Library.

Acknowledgements
Capstone Press, 6; FLPA: Alain Compost/Biosphoto, 7 Top, 11 Bottom, 28; Minden Pictures: Anup Shah, 1, 8, 13, Cyril Ruoso, 18, Konrad Wothe, 19, Suzi Eszterhas, 29 Bottom; Shutterstock: Creativa Images, Cover Back, Eric Isselee, Cover Top Left, Cover Bottom Right, hadkhanong, 27, jeep2499, Cover Top Right, Kjersti Joergensen, 15, 17, 22, Matej Hudovernik, 4, 7 Bottom Right, Michael Steden, Cover Bottom Left, Nagel Photography, 7 Bottom Left, Peter Wollinga, 12, Rich Carey, 26 Bottom, Rigamondis, Design Element, Sergey Uryadnikov, 10, 30, tristan tan, 29 Top; Thinkstock: Anup Shah, 21, Arturo Limon, 26 Top, edenwithin, 14, Eric Gevaert, 20, Eugene Junying Sim, 23, GlobalP, 32, Goddard_Photography, 5, 25, istock, 9, Marci Paravia, 16, Mickrick, 24, Zoonar RF, 11 Top.

We would like to thank Jackie Gai, DVM, for her invaluable help in the preparation of this book.

Every effort has been made to contact copyright holders of material reproduced in this book. Any omissions will be rectified in subsequent printings if notice is given to the publisher.

Contents

Amazing orangutans

Not all large animals in a rainforest live on the ground. Sometimes you have to look up. That's where orangutans spend most of their time. They are the largest animals living in the treetops.

Great apes

Orangutans are found only in south-east Asia. They live on two islands – Sumatra and Borneo.

Asia

● where orangutans live

Orangutans are great apes. This group includes chimpanzees, bonobos and gorillas. Animals in this group are clever. Some can use tools to find food. Others can grasp items with their hands and feet.

Orangutans have shaggy red fur. That's why some people call them red apes.

Male orangutans don't look the same as females. They are much larger. Males have fatty cheek pads on the sides of their faces. Pouches hang from their throats. Some males even grow beards.

Male orangutans can weigh more than 91 kilograms (200 pounds). They can measure more than 1.2 metres (4 feet) tall. Because of their size, males travel on the ground more often than females.

Up in the trees

Female orangutans can weigh up to 45 kilograms (100 pounds). They stand about 0.9 metres (3 feet) tall.

Female orangutans build nests in trees.
They make nests out of branches and leaves.
Females share the nests with their young.

Orangutans have long arms. When standing up straight, an orangutan can touch the ground with its hands. A male can stretch its arms 2.1 metres (7 feet) wide, from fingertip to fingertip.

Orangutans are very strong. They can hang from a tree branch by just one hand.

Fruit and insects

Munch! Munch! Orangutans are omnivores. They eat plants and other animals. But orangutans mainly eat plants. They climb around the forest looking for fruit. If they can't find fruit, orangutans will eat leaves and bark. Orangutans will also eat ants, caterpillars and termites. They may even eat fish.

Male orangutans spend most of their time alone. Males have territories where they search for food. To keep other males out of its territory, a male orangutan will shout. This shout can be heard more than 1.6 kilometres (1 mile) away. Males also call out to nearby females when it's time to mate.

Growing up

A female orangutan usually gives birth to one baby at a time. For the first year of its life, a baby orangutan clings to its mother. It is not strong enough to climb through the trees on its own. After about two years, it will begin to play and swing on trees.

A young orangutan spends seven to eight years with its mother. During this time it learns what to eat and how to stay safe.

Even after it has left its mother, a young orangutan may stay close to other orangutans. It watches them to learn how to behave.

Saving orangutans

Orangutans can live for up to 40 years in the wild. Because orangutans live in trees, they are safe from most predators. The only time orangutans are in danger is when they are on the ground. Then a tiger could pounce on them.

Humans are the biggest danger to orangutans. People chop down trees and destroy forests where orangutans live. They may also turn the forests into farmland. Some people even capture young orangutans to sell as pets.

Many people want to save orangutans. Wildlife groups work to protect them. In some countries there are laws against selling orangutans as pets. Parklands have been created so that orangutans can live safely. Hopefully these awesome apes will always swing through the treetops.

Glossary

cheek pad fold of skin on an animal's face

mate join together to produce young

omnivore animal that eats plants and other animals

parkland land with trees and bushes that is, or could be, used as a park

pouch flap of skin that looks like a pocket

predator animal that hunts other animals for food

termite ant-like insect that eats wood

territory area of land that an animal claims as its own to live in

Books

Animals in Danger in Asia, Richard and Louise Spilsbury (Raintree, 2013)

Introducing Asia (Introducing Continents), Anita Ganeri (Raintree, 2014)

Orangutan (A Day in the Life: Rainforest Animals), Anita Ganeri (Raintree, 2011)

Websites

www.bbc.co.uk/nature/life/Orangutan
Learn all about orangutans.

http://gowild.wwf.org.uk/asia
Find out fun facts about Asian animals, read stories and play games!

www.orangutans-sos.org/kids
Test your knowledge of orangutans by taking a quiz and completing a wordsearch.

Comprehension questions

1. Orangutans are great apes. Name two other animals that belong to this group.

2. Orangutans are omnivores. What does it mean to be an omnivore?

3. Turn to page 28. Describe what you think is happening in this photo. Use the text to help you with your answer.

Index